# A *Bundle* of Beasts

# A *Bundle* of Beasts

Patricia Hooper

*Illustrated by Mark Steele*

Houghton Mifflin Company   Boston

*Library of Congress Cataloging-in-Publication Data*

Hooper, Patricia, 1941–
   A bundle of beasts.

   Bibliography: p.
   Summary: Poems derived from old collective
nouns for animals, such as "a murder of crows"
and "a leap of leopards." Includes an explanatory
note about these terms.
   1. Animals—Juvenile poetry.   2. English language—
Collective nouns—Juvenile poetry.   3. Children's
poetry, American.   [1. Animals—Poetry.   2. American
poetry.   3. English language—Terms and phrases]
I. Steele, Mark, ill.   II. Title.
PS3558.059B8   1987        811'.54        86–34413
ISBN  0-395-44259-1
PA ISBN 0-395-61620-4

Printed in the United States of America

BP   10   9   8   7   6   5   4   3   2

# A *Bundle* of Beasts

# A *Table* of Contents

*These collective nouns, although seldom used, are correct terms for describing the following groups of animals:*

A *Drift* of Hogs                        8

A *Trip* of Goats                       10

A *Skein* of Wildfowl                   12

A *Gaggle* of Geese                     14

A *Knot* of Toads                       16

A *Parliament* of Owls                  18

A *Shrewdness* of Apes                  20

A *Smack* of Jellyfish                  22

A *Pride* of Lions                      23

A *Bouquet* of Pheasants                26

A *Clowder* of Cats                     28

A *Crash* of Rhinoceros                 30

A *Singular* of Boars                   32

A *Murder* of Crows                     33

A *Cast* of Hawks                       34

A *Leap* of Leopards                    36

An *Army* of Frogs                 40

A *Building* of Rooks              42

A *Pod* of Whales                  44

A *Charm* of Finches               45

A *Bed* of Oysters                 46

A *Route* of Wolves                48

A *Watch* of Nightingales          51

A *Band* of Gorillas               52

A *Sleuth* of Bears                54


Author's Note                      58

Suggested Reading                  60

For John, Katie, and John—P.H.

*For Emily and Georgia—M.S.*

# A *Drift* of Hogs

What's drifting ashore?

Not seaweed, not shells,
Not buoys, not bells,
Not notes in a bottle
Or ducks that can waddle—
It's hogs!

How did they get in the sea?

Some say they were in a canoe
When it tilted and sent them askew.
Some say they were surfing. Some say
They were fishing and floated away.

I say it's unclear,
But they're here—

All bellies and snouts and all squeals,
They certainly couldn't be seals;
Not dolphins, not dogs,
Not fishes, not frogs,

But they sun and they shift—
Look out, they're adrift!
It's hogs!

# A *Trip* of Goats

Have you ever taken a trip of goats?
They travel on trains and they travel on boats,
And each has a suitcase to carry his oats.
O it's lovely to travel together!

For goats wouldn't think of just walking to town
When the trains are on time and the roads are run-down,
And they know if they swam they'd be certain to drown,
So they ride when they travel together!

They chew on their cuds with their hooves in the air,
And they twiddle their beards till the passengers stare,
And you'll say to your sister, "This just isn't fair!
These goats shouldn't travel together!"

So you mustn't expect one to offer a seat,
And heaven forbid if he ventures to eat,
For a goat, you will find, isn't dainty or neat,
And they dine when they travel together!

# A *Skein* of Wildfowl

Whenever Grandma sits she knits.
The things she knits would give you fits.

She knits me sweaters, scarves, and socks.
I have to lock them in a box.

I have to sit upon the lid—
You won't believe what Grandma did!

When yarn was scarce about the house,
She spun herself a skein of grouse,

Of partridge, pheasant, geese, and quail.
She had to spin them head to tail!

12

She knit me socks and scarves and sweaters
And sent them to me like her letters.

I put them on—the day was cool—
I wish I hadn't gone to school,

For though they looked like lovely things,
They soon began to flap their wings!

They soon began to flit and flutter,
And I began to scream and stutter!

I wrote to thank her just today,
But half of them have flown away!

# A *Gaggle* of Geese

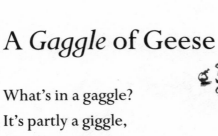

What's in a gaggle?
It's partly a giggle,
It's kind of a waggle,
It's sort of a wiggle.

It's sometimes a straggle
And always a toddle
And often a struggle
And surely a waddle.

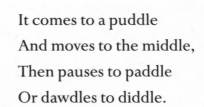

It comes to a puddle
And moves to the middle,
Then pauses to paddle
Or dawdles to diddle.

14

It swims with a squiggle
And drifts with a dabble,
Or struts with a jiggle
And gathers to gabble.

It threatens to topple
And fiddles with trouble,
Then drifts on a ripple
And blows you a bubble.

It hops with a hobble
Completely unstable,
Yet rarely will wobble
When served at the table.

# A *Knot* of Toads

Come down to the creek and see what I've found!
It leaps in the air, it hops on the ground,
It wiggles and wriggles and jiggles around,
And it croaks—it's the loveliest, throatiest sound—
And it's tied like a rope, but it's coming unbound.
It must be a knot of toads!

16

Come down to the creek where the clear waters run.
There's a game being played in the heat of the sun.
There's the heartiest laughter, the heftiest fun,
For *hundreds* of something are rolled into one,
And it's tangled . . . but hurry! It's coming undone!
It must be a knot of toads!

# A *Parliament* of Owls

What is it that astutely scowls,
Presiding over other fowls?
It is a parliament of owls.

They perch intently on their twigs
In flowing robes and powdered wigs
And nibble apricots and figs.

But when they gather for a cause,
Perhaps interpreting the laws,
They point discreetly with their claws.

And when they counsel and debate
Which birds should sing and which should mate
And which should sit upon a plate,

They listen to each argument
And shake their heads, or nod assent,
But never is an owl content

Without a place in parliament.

# A *Shrewdness* of Apes

Consider the amazing apes!
They come in such fantastic shapes:

Gorillas swinging on their bars,
And chimpanzees in foreign cars;

Orangutans, baboons, and gibbons
Wearing furs and fancy ribbons.

You find them waiting at the zoo.
You're watching them. They're watching you!

And when you pass them in their cages,
They grab their books and turn the pages;

They rev their cars or start to cook—
Just anything to make you look!

And when you look, they get their kicks:
They sit and stare and stop their tricks.

You ask for more and beg them, "Please!"
Then toss them peanuts on your knees!

They yawn and answer, acting shrewd,
"We do the tricks: you bring the food!"

# A *Smack* of Jellyfish

Have you ever felt how a jellyfish kisses?
He aims for your cheek, but be glad if he misses!

For when you're out floating, he gathers a group,
And they flop through the ocean like oysters in soup.

And just when you're drifting alone on your back,
They rise to the surface and sting with a smack!

So when you're out swimming and notice this bunch,
Just head for the beach and pretend to have lunch,

For they bobble and bubble and blow with a hiss,
And they never give up till they catch you to kiss!

# A *Pride* of Lions

When I woke him, the lion replied,
"There is something I ought to confide.
I am pleased that you came.
For a lion, I'm tame,
But you'd better not threaten my pride!"

I said to the lion, "See here!
I know I have nothing to fear,
For you're curled like a kitten
Or sloppy old mitten
And really are terribly dear."

Said the lion, "I mean what I said.
When a lion is flopped in his bed,
He looks gentle and sweet,
But a lion must eat,
And I haven't been properly fed."

I replied, "You have beautiful fur.
If I listened, I know you would purr.
Though you seem quite precocious,
You're hardly ferocious
And haven't the strength for a *grrr* . . . ."

Then the lion rose up from his rest
And said, "You are failing the test!
You must leave in a hurry,
I beg you to scurry
For I fear there's a roar in my chest!"

But I asked, "May I give you a pat?
I'll trade you my gloves and my hat.
I'm hardly afraid
Of the stir you have made.
Like your friends, you're a chubby old cat!"

24

Then the lion let loose with a roar
And cried, as I fled through the door,
"You must run! You must hide!
You've insulted my pride!
You must never wake *me* anymore!"

# A *Bouquet* of Pheasants

How lovely, in a living room,
To keep a vase where pheasants bloom,
All plumes and feathered fronds!

How fine to fetch them from a field
And find the slender stems revealed
And carry them like wands!

What joy to set them in the sink
As if they might consent to drink
From artificial ponds!

26

And then to tuck them in a vase
Like blossoms oddly out of place
In such restrictive bonds!

What fun to make them such a nest
And then present them to a guest
To see how she responds!

# A *Clowder*\*of Cats

What would you do with a clowder of cats?
I'd take them to breakfast and buy them all hats.

I'd join them for luncheon and comb out their tresses
And give them gold bracelets and dress them in dresses.

\**Clowder* = clutter

I'd meet them for tea at the fanciest places
And ruffle their whiskers and kiss all their faces.

I'd ask them to dinner and serve them clam chowder,
Then clean up the kitchen and clear out the clowder!

29

# A *Crash* of Rhinoceros

What *is* that climbing up my stair?
It's not a boar. It's not a bear.

It jiggles like a pile of junk.
It's leathery as someone's trunk.

It's ponderous and has a pout,
And on its pout it has a snout,

And on its snout it has a horn
As odd as any unicorn.

It's frivolous and flubbery
And boisterous and blubbery!

But wait! There must be three or four
Who've wobbled through my kitchen door!

They climb the stair, and sway, and stop,
Then balance bravely at the top—

The end, of course, is obvious,
And though it seems preposterous,

The crash is of rhinoceros!

# A *Singular* of Boars

The boar is a peculiar pig.
He's known as something of a prig.

He bristles at the slightest glance
And rarely condescends to dance.

He locks his door and keeps the key
And never comes in time for tea.

And when he's greeted, though he hears,
He won't reply for years and years.

So *flock* and *herd* are excellent
When other groups are what is meant.

They stand for plurals that occur.
But boars are always singular.

# A *Murder* of Crows

Over the river it's flying,
Over the mountain it goes.
You can tell from its cawing and crying,
It must be a murder of crows.

Its wings make an ominous roaring,
It's black as a midnight of storms,
And over the city it's soaring,
And over the rooftop it swarms.

It's raucous and rushing and screaming,
A sinister wind overhead.
But what is it plotting and scheming?
—I'm glad that I'm safe in my bed!

# A *Cast* of Hawks

"Come and sit," said the hawks.
"We are giving a play."

"In your house?" asked the mouse.
"But I really can't stay."

"In your lair?" asked the hare.
"But it's getting quite late."

"In your den?" asked the wren.
"But I see you've a plate!"

"Come and see," said the hawks.
"We are giving a show."

"Just for us?" asked the mouse.
"Well, perhaps. Maybe so."

"I'll be there," said the hare.
"But I wish you were storks."

"Don't go in," cried the wren,
"For I see they have forks!"

"Please applaud," said the hawks,
"And we'll start to perform."

"Our applause," said the mouse,
"Couldn't do any harm."

"Do we dare?" asked the hare.
"Then the play shall begin!"

"Must the actors wear bibs?
We must run!" cried the wren.

# A *Leap* of Leopards

The leopard in his leotard
Addressed the burly bear.
He said, "I have to practice hard
For leaping in the air."
The bear replied, "I'd rather knit
While sitting in my chair."

The leopard practiced pirouettes,
For he adored ballet.
He said, "To learn to leap from nets,
I'll start with a plié."
The bear replied, "That seems to me
A silly thing to say!"


The leopard taught his friends to leap;
His reputation grew.
He said, "Such expertise will keep
All leopards from the zoo."
The bear replied, "I'd rather knit
Than leap around like you!"


The leopard heard the hunt begin
And donned his dancing clothes.
He said, "This is the sort of thing
That keeps me on my toes!"
The bear sat knitting in his chair
And welcomed in his foes!

He said, "I'm sure that you have come
To catch the dancing cat.
He's giving lessons in my home;
He used to be quite fat.
All winter long those leopards leapt
While I just sat and sat."

The leopard heard him tell the tale
And said, "We mustn't stay!"
And while the hunters turned quite pale,
He did a grand jeté!
The bear sat knitting with a smile.
The leopards leapt away!

But while the hunters stood in shock,
The bear rose up and threw
His knitting, like a giant sock,
About the startled crew,
And put them in a pot and said,
"I'll knit—you make the stew!"

# An *Army* of Frogs

Don't ever jog
Alone in a bog
Unless you're prepared
To meet up with a frog
In his army-green suit,
For he's ready to shoot
With his long, sticky tongue
If you fail to salute!

He marches and drills,
He croaks and he trills
With his fly-catching comrades
Who'll give you the chills!
They drum and they thump
Till the lily pads jump,
And they hop to the path
And they land with a

                BUMP!

Right where you're standing
An army is landing!
Salute (or they'll shoot!)
And then—scoot!

# A *Building* of Rooks

To build a building out of rooks,
Begin by reading ancient books,

The kind containing charms and spells
For finding gold and hidden wells.

They'll tell you how to capture birds
By saying certain magic words,

And how to stack them smooth and flat
(Just give them each a friendly pat),

And how to make the stack be still
(Insert a cherry in each bill),

And how to place the pointed feet
(In slippers, for conserving heat),

And how to set the shining tails
(Perhaps along the roof, for sails),

And even how to spread the wings
Until, at last, your building sings!

And then, if you should move inside,
You'll know the way you ought to ride

In case it rises in the air
(Just curl up in your favorite chair).

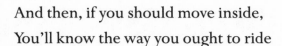

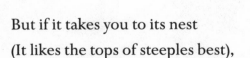

But if it takes you to its nest
(It likes the tops of steeples best),

Call out to notify the town
In case it all comes crashing down!

# A *Pod* of Whales

On a vine lived a pea in a pod full of whales.
It said to the others, "Don't wiggle your tails!"
Said the whales to the pea, "It's so hard not to squirm,
For we haven't been watered. Who *are* you? A worm?"

Said the pea to the whales, "It's so crowded, I guess
I don't really fit in, so the answer is yes."
Said the whales to the pea, "Who are we? Are we beans?"
Said the pea, "Don't be silly. You *must* be sardines!"

# A *Charm*\* of Finches

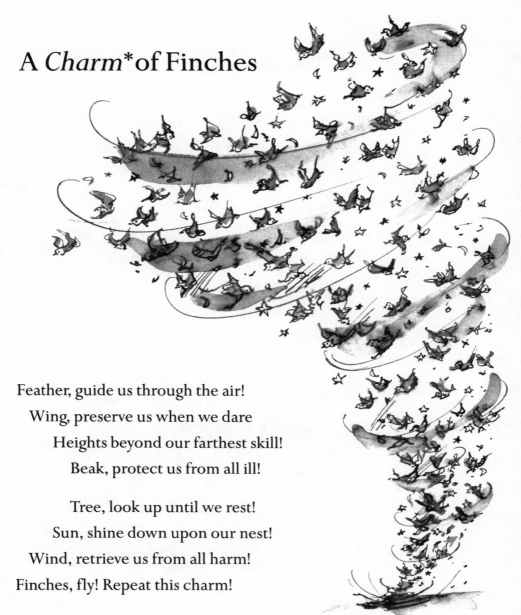

Feather, guide us through the air!
Wing, preserve us when we dare
Heights beyond our farthest skill!
Beak, protect us from all ill!

Tree, look up until we rest!
Sun, shine down upon our nest!
Wind, retrieve us from all harm!
Finches, fly! Repeat this charm!

\* *Charm* = magic spell.

# A *Bed* of Oysters

"Good night," said my mother, and put out the light.
"Good night," said a voice in the dark of the night.
I looked, and an oyster was saying good night!

It sat with its sisters on top of my quilt.
It said, "When you landed, you gave us a tilt,
For you see, we've been here since this bed was first built!"

I said, "But today it was given to me.
It's time you went back to your bed in the sea."
The oysters looked angry. They didn't agree.

"This bed is much nicer," the first oyster said,
"And that is the reason we chose it instead.
For you know that an oyster *must* live in a bed."

I said, "But this morning it came like the mail.
My grandmother sent it; she bought it on sale.
And oysters, forgive me, belong in a pail."

Then they slipped and they slithered and slid to my feet.
They said, "You'll be sorry we happened to meet!"
—Now I'm under the bed, and they're under the sheet!

# A *Route* of Wolves

The wolves lay down in the grass.
They said, "We are making a road!
When the rabbits come by,
How still we shall lie!"
And the moon in the melon tree glowed.

The rabbits came by in the dark.
They were looking for raspberry buns
Which were said to have grown
When the melon tree shown
By the light of the lavender sun.
"O where are the raspberry buns?" they asked,
"And when will our searching be done?"

48

Then they noticed a road through the woods
And a signpost that pointed the way.
"Let us follow the trail
That begins like a tail
And return to the lavender day!"

So the wolves held their breath and lay low.
How tickly the tramping of feet!
It was certainly more
Than the wolves could ignore,
Yet they all lay as still as a street!
"How tickly the tramping of feet!" thought the wolves.
"What delectable morsels to eat!"

But the rabbits continued to bounce
For the path was as thick as a bed.
"It is rather like fur
And it started to stir
When I touched it," the first rabbit said.

Then another, who followed behind,

Said, "It's softer than sand, I suppose.

And at times it appears

That it even has ears,

For I've felt them with each of my toes!"

"Will it lead us to raspberry buns?" asked one.

"Will it ever reveal where it goes?

Will it suddenly rise

With a glint in its eyes

While the moon in the melon tree glows?"

And they leapt with a bound

Without turning around

When they noticed a twitch of its nose!

There were raspberry buns

In the lavender sun,

But they ran when they noticed its nose!

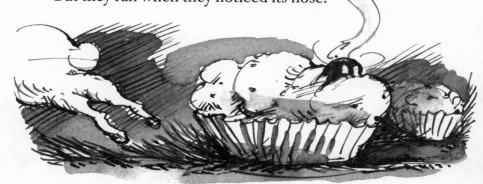

# A *Watch* of Nightingales

I rarely know the proper time:
The watch I wear will never chime.

It never chimes, it only sings.
It points the hour with its wings.

And though it tells the date and weather,
It hides them each beneath a feather.

So when I lay me down to rest,
I lay my watch upon its nest.

I only hope my watch will lay
An ordinary watch some day!

# A *Band* of Gorillas

A band of gorillas is coming to town.
They dangle from treetops and drum upside down.
They clang with their cymbals and strum with their feet,
But you'd better watch out if they come down your street!

They tune up their trumpets and toot out their tunes,
They blow on their bugles and blare their bassoons.
But if you look friendly, they'll march through your door,
Straight over your sofa, and camp on the floor!

They'll pound your piano and tweedle their flutes,
They'll twang on your fiddle and stomp with their boots.
They're loud as hyenas and wild as chinchillas—
Don't ever make friends with a band of gorillas!

# A *Sleuth* of Bears

When something's lost and I'm in bed
I sometimes hear bears coming.
I watch the window shade blow in
And hear a distant humming.

It's hard to sleep when others keep
Such oddly different hours.
I lie awake again and wait.
They march through mother's flowers,

And then right up the garden path
And through the halls they're walking.
I hardly breathe—the curtain stirs,
And then I see them stalking.

They carry flashlights in their hands
And shine them on the ceiling.
They search the floors and dresser drawers,
And then my mind goes reeling—

For these are bears that hunt through chairs!
The largest of them hovers
Above my bed and shakes his head
And pats the lumpy covers.

And then they bow and seem to blow
Apart like papa's sneezes.
I hear them pass across the grass
And fade like morning breezes.


Then all my room's a buzzing hive
As though they'd come for honey,
And right away I know next day
I'm going to find my money,


My socks, my old library card,
My tooth that missed the fairy,
My fishing hooks, my comic books,
My pen, my pet canary.


For when they come, they turn up things
I must have left behind me,
And when I'm lost, I'll simply wish:
I know that bears will find me.

# Author's Note

Where did the names for groups of animals come from? Nearly everyone has heard of a *school* of fish, yet there was a time when this term was probably no more or less common than a *knot* of toads or a *leap* of leopards. In fact, certain fifteenth-century manuscripts known as Books of Courtesy contained long lists of these terms, the knowledge of which was expected of English gentlemen. Long ago, when the English language was still young, the desire to refer properly to different groups of animals resulted in the invention of many delightful phrases based, for example, on the way animals looked, what they did, how they sounded, or simply on whimsical comparisons which the animals in gatherings evoked.

Of course, the pictures we see when we hear these terms are not always those intended by their inventors. The *Oxford English Dictionary* lists both a *sleuth* and a *sloth* for a company of bears, and both words originally meant "laziness". Still, *sleuth*-hounds were used to track criminals as early as the Middle Ages; and what visitor to Yellowstone, having had a picnic detected by bears, would not argue that *sleuth*, in its detective sense, is at least as appropriate to bears as *sloth*? A *drift* was intended for animals being driven along, not drifting about in water; a *trip*, according to the *Oxford English Dictionary*, was probably related to "troop" rather than "journey"; and a *cast* referred to a pair of hawks released simultaneously by a falconer, not to a group of actors. Yet certain other terms—a *shrewdness* of apes, for example— probably awakened the same images in the minds of their first audiences as they do in ours.

My wish was to be faithful not to the original meanings of these terms, but to whatever pictures occurred to me on first hearing such wonderful phrases. I remember hearing of a *clowder* (clutter) of cats and realizing how similar it was to a term I had often heard but never thought about, a *litter* of puppies! When listed beside terms as unusual and striking as a *bouquet* of pheasants or a *pod* of whales, phrases as familiar as a *school* of fish or a *team* of horses begin to reclaim the freshness they must have had for the long-forgotten inventors of these terms. When words are seen in a new context, the dust of familiarity is brushed away, and the metaphors, shining, become new.

Through the years, other terms have been added to those which appeared in print over five hundred years ago, and many have changed or fallen into disuse. However, they are all recorded in various dictionaries, thesauri, and histories of language, and if you would like to know more about these and many other surprising but perfectly appropriate names for groups of animals, you might enjoy reading about them in some of the following books.

# Suggested Reading

Adams, J. Donald. *The Magic and Mystery of Words.* New York: Holt, Rinehart & Winston, 1963.

Hendrickson, Robert. *Animal Crackers.* New York: Viking, 1983.

Laughlin, William H. *Laughlin's Fact Finder.* West Nyack, New York: Parker Publishing, 1969.

Lipton, James. *An Exaltation of Larks.* New York: Grossman, 1968.

Morris, William and Mary. *A Dictionary of Word and Phrase Origins.* New York: Harper & Row, 1962.